# POP SMOKE

# LIFE DOCUMENTARY

# & MEMOIR

## (Death Revelation and Tribute of

## The Stars)

### Biography of the Rap Legend

# Pop Smoke

# Table of Contents

# INTRODUCTION

Bashar Barakah Jackson (July 20, 1999 - February 19, 2020), referred to and known as Pop Smoke, was an American rapper, musician and songwriter. He was viewed by quite a few people to be the figure of Brooklyn drill. Brought up in Canarsie, Brooklyn, Pop Smoke started his musical profession in late 2018 with his single "MPR (Panic 3 Remix)". Pop Smoke rose to spotlight with the dropping of his breakout singles *"Welcome to the Party"* and *"Dior"* in 2019. He frequently teamed up with UK drill producers and performers, who utilized more aggressive and forceful instrumentation than drill artists from Chicago.

## Factual Data

Birth Name: Bashar Barakah Jackson

Date Of Birth: July 20, 1999

Place Of Birth: New York City, U.S.

Died: February 19, 2020 (20 years of age)

Place Of Birth: Los Angeles, California, U.S.

Genres:  • Hip Hop

   • Brooklyn drill

- R&B

Occupation: • Rapper

• Song Writer

• Vocalist

Labels: • Victor Victor

• Republic

Place Buried: Green-Wood Graveyard in Brooklyn, New York

# CHAPTER ONE

## Early life

Bashar Barakah Jackson (Pop Smoke) was conceived on July 20, 1999, in Brooklyn, New York City, to a Jamaican mother, Audrey Jackson, and a Panamanian dad, Greg Jackson. Obasi is his elder brother. Jackson was bred in Canarsie, an area in southeast Brooklyn, He went to nine distinct schools during his childhood in Canarsie, Brooklyn.

He played the African drums in his neighborhood church as a kid, Sometimes he played drums by hand at chapel, yet for the most part he played sports: At 15, Jackson was a sufficiently skilled basket ball player to win an awarded scholarship to a private academy in Philadelphia. However, his visit to Philadelphia was brief. An occurrence long sent Jackson back to Brooklyn which was undisclosed, he started to get some cash of his own that he purchased a BMW 5 Series when he was just 16.

Jackson was given an expulsion from eighth grade for carrying a pistol to school and penalized with two years on house arrest in the charges labeled for having a weapon. Jackson began playing base-ball as a point and shooting guard. He moved to Philadelphia to sign up for Rock-top Institute. He was prompt to leave when he developed a heart disease, and Jackson in the end went to what I call "The Street Lifestyle".

## BEGINING OF CAREER

Around the ending of the year 2018, Jackson (pop smoke) was surfing instrumentals on YouTube and listened to a beat called "Panic." It had been produced by *808 Melo* who is also a producer, and had recently worked with *Sheff G*, a musician on the main edge of Brooklyn drill. Their relationship grew sporadically, which made Pop Smoke fly Melo from east London to Brooklyn, for a collaboration which gave rise to *"Meet the Woo"*. It was then that Jackson started sharpening his melodic signature, a voice so intense and gravelly as to be an instrument. Perhaps his greatest hit includes a Chorus that disintegrates, in a real sense, into a drifted growl.

In a meeting, he expressed that his performing name of Pop Smoke is a mix of *Poppa*, a name given to him by his Panamanian grandma, and *Smocco Guwop*, a nickname from cherished, lifelong friends and it was likewise his old Instagram name. On January 28, 2019, he dropped *"Flexin"*. Jackson got to know Rico Beats the producer, who was familiar with the record chief, Steven Victor.

The three set up a meeting, and in April 2019, Jackson signed to Victor Victor and Republic Records. On April 23, 2019, Jackson dropped his breakout single, *"Welcome to the Party"*, that was created by 808Melo. Numerous remixes of the melody were subsequently recorded, with the industrially dropped versions featured by *Nicki Minaj* and the other including *Skepta*. Jackson dropped his mixtape *"Meet the Woo"* on July 26, 2019. From October to December 2019, Jackson dropped numerous singles, including *"War"* with *Lil Tjay*, and *"100k on a Coupe"* with *Calboy*. On December 27, 2019, Jackson showed up on *Travis Scott's* Cactus Jack Records collection album JackBoys on the music *"Gatti"* which was likewise joined by the music video. "Gatti" appeared and topped at number 69 on the US Billboard Hot 100, giving Jackson his most memorable Hot 100 appearance. On January 16, 2020, Jackson dropped "Christopher Walking". On February 7, 2020, Jackson dropped his second mix-tape *Meet the Woo 2*, featuring *Quavo, A Boogie wit da Hoodie, Fivio Foreign* and *Lil Tjay*.

The mixtape appeared at number seven on the US Announcement Billboard 200, acquiring Jackson his most memorable top-10 hit in the US. Five days after its has been dropped, a version was released with three new music, each featuring a guest, comprising of *Nav*, *Gunna*, and *PnB Rock*. Jackson shook the social media with his concert tour *["Meet the Woo Tour"]* enabling him promote the two mix-tapes of his. The visit was scheduled to start in the US and end in the UK within a month.

## CAREER BROUGHT TO LIGHT

"Dior", the subsequent single of Meet the Woo, turned into Jackson's most listened solo hit, topping at number 22 on the Announcement Billboard Hot 100 and number 33 on the UK Singles Top Chart. Toward the start of the month of march 2020, American rapper 50-Cent posted on his Instagram that he had chosen to create and complete Jackson's studio collection and album solely. After his declaration, 50 Cent called musicians like *Roddy Ricch*, *Drake*, and *Chris Brown* intending to feature them on the record. Pop Smoke had intended to take his mom to an entertainment Award show inciting *50 Cent* to vow to take her to one when the album collection was finished.

## Pop Smoke

On April 16, 2020, a narrative on Pop Smoke's life was reported to be in progress. On May 14, 2020, Victor reported that Pop Smoke's studio album collection would be dropped on June 12, 2020. The album collection would be known as Shoot for the Stars, Aim for the Moon. It was initially set for dropping on June 12, 2020, yet was pushed back keeping in mind the George Floyd fights. On the album original release date, the lead single, *"Make It Rain"*, featured by Brooklyn rapper *Rowdy Rebel* was dropped rather.

Rebel's part was recorded through a call since he was on detention at that point. *Virgil Abloh* made the album collection's unique cover. The cover art design incited huge critics from fans who referred to it as "pathetic" and "unprofessional" and felt it was unacceptable. It incited a Change request drawing in huge number of petitions. *Ryder Ripps* made the last cover design with the chrome rose against a dark foundation. Jackson's mom picked the last album collection cover hours before the album was made publicly.

The album was dropped officially on July 3, 2020, to publicity success, arriving at number one in most countries, even on the Announcement Billboard 200. Each of the 19 songs on the album collection graphed on the Billboard Hot 100, with "For the Evening" featured by *Lil Baby* and *DaBaby*, appearing at number six, giving Pop Smoke his first top-10 hit in quite a while. On July 20, 2020, on what might have been Jackson's 21st birthday, an exclusive version of the album was dropped, and included 15 new extra tracks. The album collection's fifth single *"What You Know about Love"*, later ended up cresting at number nine on the Billboard Hot 100, giving Pop Smoke his second top-10 hit in the US. On February 26, 2021, "AP" was dropped as the lead single for the Boogie soundtrack. Pop Smoke was given a role as a monk in a minor role for the Boogie movie.

A second album collection named Faith was dropped on July 16, 2021. It appeared at number one on the Billboard 200.

## Relationship and Personal Life

Before he died, Pop Smoke was involved in a relationship with model *Alyssa Danielle*. Pop smoke had tried not to discuss his relationship life, yet after he died, Alyssa affirmed that she was dating the rap legend.

She uncovered that Pop was hesitant about dating, yet he in the long run surrendered. She

## Pop Smoke

discussed the Valentine's Day gift that Pop smoke gave her and the couple's relationship progress since January 2020.

It is an obscure, yet interesting bit of trivia Pop's relationship with *Jakeilah Orti* yielded him a child. Ortiz and the kid went to Pop's memorial service, however she wanted a paternity test confirmation before declaring that he is Pop's child.

# CHAPTER TWO

## Legal issues

Drill was bred in Chicago, where it was stunning for its honesty: The rhymes points out wrongdoings and its consequence, material and mental, in clear terms. While drill lives on in Chicago and has been through other rap scenes in the U.S, the scene in Brooklyn is the main American one to adhere the style to another new locale. Jackson's music specifically has an extraordinary approach to reconfiguring the maximalist sounds of early and mid-2000s.

When *"Meet the Woo"* dropped, by then *"Welcome to the Party"* had already turned into a famous music. It topped at No. 9 on the Hot 100 and got a *Nicki Minaj* remix.

While police violently targeted rappers, drill music appears to have gotten under police's skin lowkey. *Keef*, a fellow Rap star, has for some time been prohibited from entertaining in his native Chicago area, and London police targeted rappers due to censorship related acts. This also applied to Jackson (pop smoke).

In October, he was to play the First New York version of the famous rap celebration Rolling

Loud. In the morning the celebration was to start, it prompted an NYPD solicitation to pull Jackson, alongside four other drill nearby rappers (*Sheff G, Casanova, 22Gz,* and *Don Q*), from the bill, referring to "public safety concerns" and asserting — without charges or proof — that the five had "been linked with violence actions." Law enforcement in New York later deliberated that Jackson was linked with a Crip set; when Rolling Loud was cancelled, he was not accused of any Crimes.

On January 17, 2020, when coming back from Paris Fashion Week, Jackson was captured by Federal agents at John F. Kennedy Airport for a stolen Rolls-Royce Phantom issue, worth over $375,000, whose owner filed a stolen report case after Jackson had supposedly rented it in California for a music video shoot on the condition it would be returned the following day. Detectives believed he planned out for the vehicle to be moved on a flatbed truck to New York. He posted a photograph of himself before the stolen vehicle on his Instagram page including Facebook. The vehicle was found by authorities at Jackson's mom's home, in the Canarsie part of Brooklyn. After his capture, police investigated him concerning a minor shooting that occurred in Brooklyn in June 2019. The police thought he had data on the shooting because he was caught on camera driving a vehicle reversing from the exact location of the crime. The police likewise attempted to pressure Jackson into enlightening them more on data concerning the Crips, GS9, and other Brooklyn gangsters, however he would not talk. He was charged with car robbery, and accepted to avoid known gangsters and submit drug tests to the US pretrial administrations. The circumstances Jackson was put under ruined some of his shows like the *"BK Drip Concert"* at a place known as Kings Theater in Flatbush in February 2020, as fellow gang members would be among the crowd.

## Death

On February 19, 2020, Jackson rented a house through Airbnb whose owner is The Real Housewives star *Teddi Mellencamp* and her partner, *Edwin Arroyave*, in Hollywood Hills, California. The day preceding his murder, Jackson (pop smoke) and a friend of his *Michael Durodola* had posted a few pictures on their Social Media handles, also adding one for which Mellencamp's residence address was visible in the background. The rapper likewise posted a story on Instagram and Facebook of presents he received. One showed the house's full location and address on the package.

At around 4:30 a.m., five hooded men, including one wearing a ski mask and holding a pistol, broke into the house through a balcony of the second-story while Jackson was taking his bath. The robbers held a pistol to a lady's head and vowed to kill her. Few seconds later, the lady heard the men shoot Jackson multiple times after hearing struggles.

The LAPD got fresh insight about the home intrusion from a call from the East Coast. Police showed up at the home six minutes after and found Jackson with numerous gunshots wounds. He was conveyed to Cedars-Sinai Hospital, where doctors did a thoracotomy on the left part of his chest. A couple of hours after the incident, he was confirmed dead. He was just 20 years of age. On February 21, the Los Angeles Division of Medical Examine; Coroner made known that the reason for Jackson's demise was a bullet shot in the torso.

The LAPD at first thought that Jackson's death was gang related as he was attached to the Crips. After several investigations were carried out, the LAPD later accepted his death was the outcome of a home robbery turned out wrong. It was known that the robbers took Jackson's gold watch and other expensive jewelries before taking off from the house.

## Pop Smoke

On July 9, 2020, three adult men and two minors were captured for the homicide of the rapper. One of the grown-up suspects has been accused of homicide with an extraordinary situation that identified the killing was committed "during the operation of a robbery and a burglary", and the other accused of attempted murder. The two adolescents have been accused of homicide and burglary in juvenile court.

In May 2021, a 15-year-old, the youngest of the four robbers, supposedly owned up to killing Jackson over a diamond encrusted Rolex during a recorded interview with a fellow prisoner at the juvenile detention place. The 15-year-old told the fellow prisoner that Jackson at first consented to their demand for the jewels however at that point attempted to fight them, and a struggle broke out in which Jackson was fired with a Beretta M9. The robbers snatched his Rolex, which they sold for $2,000.

Jackson's body was initially intended to be laid to rest at the Cypress Hills Graveyard but was later changed to Green-Wood Cemetery. Family, friends, fans of Jackson, and loved ones assembled in his old hometown of Canarsie, Brooklyn, to show their regards and pay their last respects. His coffin was pulled in a Horse drawn carriage and was encircled by glass windows and white draperies.

# CHAPTER THREE

## AWARDS WON

| 2020 | BET Hip Hop Awards | Best New Hip Hop Artist | Won |
|------|--------------------|-------------------------|-----|
| 2021 | Grammy Awards | Top New Artist | Won |
| 2021 | Billboard Music Awards | Top Rap Artist | Won |
| | *Shoot for the Stars, Aim for the Moon* | Top Billboard 200 album | Won |

Pop Smoke's death shocked numerous in the rap industry as well as committed fans of the exceptional legend.

## The Real Facts About Legend Pop-Smoke

Pop Smoke was a remarkable new star in Brooklyn's scene. His mixtape, "*Meet the Woo*" was released in July, and "Meet the Woo, Vol. 2" which was popular on the Billboard. "Dior" and a "*Welcome to the Party*" remix that Nicki Minaj was featured both made it into the top 50 on Billboard's rundown of hot R&B/hip-hop tunes. "Gatti," which featured Pop Smoke alongside Travis Scott, broke the main 35 on that chart.

**He played the 2019 Rolling Loud celebration festival in Los Angeles** in December, alongside *Lil Uzi Vert* and *Playboi Carti*. "*What Rolling Loud*, as a travelling occasion, addresses is the shock of the new: commotion over order, charisma over clarity, bad energies over good".

**He was one of five rappers the NYPD asked Rolling Loud to remove from its New York arrangements**. Pop Smoke, 22Gz, Casanova, Sheff G and Don Q were called out in a police letter to coordinators of the event as being "partnered with ongoing violence and savagery in the city hence Coordinators of the event obeyed and listened to the police demands.

**Pop Smoke and his group knew that their way of life brought risks and chances**. During the Brooklyn Queens Expressway, he and his group took part in what can be referred to as guarded driving acts: bending orders, irregular speeding and unnecessary parking and slowing, impeding and obstructing different vehicles from their path.

## Pop Smoke

It was the kind of conduct and act showed by the individuals who were aware that something suddenly terrible could occur to them without warning.

**He was going to go out on an international worldwide tour for a month**. Pop Smoke had two shows set for a month at the Roxy in West Hollywood, in addition to one at the Constellation Room in St Nick Ana, that would have taken him across the U.S. Likewise on schedule were shows in the U.K., Ireland, France, Belgium and Portugal.

**He was freed on $250,000 bail** prior to being detained in New York on charges of stealing a Rolls-Royce that he had rented for the time being for a music video shoot in L.A. Jackson was charged of a federalized crime, interstate shipping of a stolen vehicle, after he planned for the vehicle to be sent cross-country on a flatbed truck. He had posted a picture of himself with the $375,000 vehicle online. It was found at Jackson's mom's Brooklyn home with its plates changed and windows tinted. He involved in a redirection program for first-time lawbreakers, connected with weapons ownership.

# Mysteries and Revelations of Death

Revelations and further investigations brought up that he had posted photographs on social media showing loads of money, as well as an expensive vehicle and designers. He had likewise placed up posts on Facebook and Instagram with pictures of designer bags; the location and exact address of the rental was showing on the receipts and packages. Mike Durodola, Pop Smoke's friend, additionally posted not less than one photograph in which the location could not be fully seen — prompting a few fans and people to blame him for setting up his friend. Durodola, who was at Pop Smoke's rental during the shooting, condemned those allegations, prompting him to post on Instagram: that he couldnt have ever setup his own brother. Police additionally investigated whether Jackson's murder was connected with his acts with the Crips.

On July 9, 2020, the Los Angeles Police Division declared that it had captured five individuals involved in Pop Smoke's homicide. After four days, detectives declared that four of them were charged in Pop Smoke's murder: _Corey Walker_ (19), _Keandre Rodgers_ (18), and two minor teenagers whose names were withheld on account of their age. Although the suspects were in an L.A. gang, police sources confirmed the murder wasn't connected to Pop Smoke's potential gang cults, considering that he was from New York City, nor inclusive of a potential East Coast-West Coast conflict.

Almost a year after the incident, new evidence concerning Pop Smoke's homicide arose in court, during two days of preceding to decide if evidence against Walker would go to trial.

## Revelations on Jackson's death from the proceedings.

### *Pop Smoke's real killer was just 15 years of age.*

Los Angeles Police Division detective confirmed that Pop Smoke was lethally shot by the 15-year-old suspect. The youngsters associated with Pop Smoke's murder were supposedly at his rental to take his diamond encrusted Rolex and Cuban chain. They just ended up taking Pop Smoke's watch and later sold it for just a simple $2,000.

The shooter, who is charged with murder and robbery, "accepted that they requested the jewelry" and afterward got into "a struggle" with Pop Smoke, They got into a battle, and he shot

Jackson multiple times, The charged said he shot him on the back. These disclosures arrived in a recorded prison interview between the youngster and his fellow prisoner in May 2020.

## Walker supposedly owned up to his part in Pop Smoke's murder.

Corey Walker owned up to his part in Pop Smoke's demise during a recorded discussion with a disguise put in his prison cell. Walker, who has argued not guilty, let this disguised detective know that the robbery team wore ski masks and gloves and made use of a police scanner to do their plotted plan, with the sole aim of not to be caught. it was revealed that the suspects involved in the murder of Pop Smoke were members of a similar gang squad furthermore information about his location was from his Instagram posts.

## Pop Smoke retaliated.

Walker likewise let the disguised detective know that when the robbery team showed up at Pop Smoke's rental, they approached him when he was in the shower. Walker described that the youngsters requested Pop Smoke hands over his jewelries, which he had on in the shower.

The teen robbers thanked him when it seemed like Pop Smoke would play along to their request, unfortunately, Pop Smoke at last refused and retaliated against the robbers, which prompted the robbers to "gun whipped" him. The shooter continued to start shooting, hitting Pop Smoke in the chest.

## *Pop Smoke's companion gave information to police.*

Detailed facts were made known that a lady who was with Pop Smoke let the cops know that men on mask raged through the draperies of the balcony of second-story. Los Angeles Police Office criminal investigation affirmed that one of the robbers purportedly put a pistol against the lady's head while the others burst into the bathroom where Pop Smoke was showering.

She heard a battle coming from the shower and heard Mr. Jackson shouting. Mr. Jackson ran out of the shower and afterward she heard a loud pop and heard Mr. Jackson tumble to the ground, Pop Smoke was likewise kicked after being shot, as revealed by the female friend. Two others started to kick him; Mr. Jackson gets up and tries to run down the stairs. She hears two additional pops. She follows Mr. Jackson, sees him on the ground and shouts for Michael Durodola to call 911, The lady made the revelations after Pop Smoke's lethal shooting.

## Walker's vehicle supposedly involves him to the homicide.

Los Angeles Police Office investigation affirmed that CCTV footages attached Walker to Pop Smoke's killing. The tape showed a vehicle carrying the suspects to the scene, and the registered plate number was linked to Walker.

## Walker demanded he wasn't in Pop Smoke's rental.

Walker's legal advisor said in court that Walker never entered Pop Smoke's home yet rather stayed in his vehicle, and asked the young suspects not to start shooting. He was against the planned murder, moreover the lawyer insisted that he [walker] Probably, He's just a driver and was outside. The lawyer put forth this case trying to get Walker's murder allegation dropped.

Investigations proved that Walker had surveyed Pop Smoke's home hours before the fatal robbery. Walker was additionally mindful that different suspects were plotting to ransack Pop Smoke at gunpoint, he explicitly monitored this house to determine when the casualty will be there, investigations confirmed, and guaranteeing Walker had a wild lack of concern

## Pop Smoke

to human existence. Walker's lawyer made it clear saying, that Mr. Walker didn't kill anyone, and that his client really loved Pop Smoke.

The judge regulating Walker's case, Dirt Jacke II, dismissed walker's lawyer contention to decrease the charges. Assuming Walker is indicted on his present charges, he possibly faces death and execution penalty. While the other teen suspects were on trial awaiting in juvenile court.

# CHAPTER FOUR

## Funeral and Weird Instances

Pop Smoke's last resting place in Brooklyn was destroyed and vandalized Saturday in an obvious destructive incident.

Trash was thrown about the catacomb at Brooklyn's Green-Wood grave yard after the marble tombstone of the rapper, engraved with his name, was crushed in the fierce vandal.

The rapper's given name can be seen clearly on the messed up marble in the catacomb, Blossoms of flowers, broken stone were visible on the floor.

### TRIBUTE OF THE STARS

Pop smokes death came as a shock and broke the hearts of many including beloved fans and stars who worked with him. Tributes were written to honor Pop smoke and keep the legends memory.

- *The Bible tells us that jealousy is as cruel as the grave, Unbelievable. Rest in Peace POP {Nicki Minaj}*

- *Got to Know this Kid! Very Talented Humble Respectful and Appreciative*

  *RIP {Quavo}*

- *R.I.P to my man Pop Smoke, No sympathy for winners. God bless him {50 Cent}*

- *Rest In Power {Dr Love}*

- *R.I.P, lil homie. Damn I'm hurt all over again, Gone 2 Soon {snoop dogg}*

- *I can't believe Pop Smoke passed away. People are just so Cruel, He was only 20 years old. Please count your blessings every day, and live life to the fullest. You can be here today, and gone tomorrow {Skai}*

THE KNOWN FACT IS THE WAY PEOPLE DIE IS KEPT IN THE HEARTS OF THE LIVING.

OUR LEGENDS AREN'T DEAD IN OUR HEARTS YET, ONLY WHEN WE CHOOSE THE PATH FOR THEM TO BE FORGOTTEN.

*[SMOKEZ REPUBLIC]*

**A Book Written in the Loving Memory of Pop Smoke.**

**RIP Legend.**

Made in the USA
Las Vegas, NV
19 January 2023

65900781R00020